Moon Fire:
Poetry on Skating

poems by

Mardelle Fortier

Finishing Line Press
Georgetown, Kentucky

Moon Fire:
Poetry on Skating

Copyright © 2018 by Mardelle Fortier
ISBN 978-1-63534-765-4 First Edition
All rights reserved under International and Pan-American Copyright Conventions. No part of this book may be reproduced in any manner whatsoever without written permission from the publisher, except in the case of brief quotations embodied in critical articles and reviews.

ACKNOWLEDGMENTS

"Color of Roses" and "Gift of Ice." Poetry Pacific Press. Nov. 2016

"Lady of the Ice." *DuPage Arts and Life*. Procopian Press, Benedictine University. Sept. 2003.

Publisher: Leah Maines
Editor: Christen Kincaid
Cover Photo: Laura Vacca
Author Photo: Mary Jane Bradley-Smith
Cover Design: Leah Huete

Printed in the USA on acid-free paper.
Order online: www.finishinglinepress.com
also available on amazon.com

Author inquiries and mail orders:
Finishing Line Press
P. O. Box 1626
Georgetown, Kentucky 40324
U. S. A.

Table of Contents

Minutes of Pearl 1
Boccelli Sings; Boitano Skates 2
First Grand Prix Victory 3
Lady of the Ice 4
Flying over Paris 5
Dangerous Skate 6
Hazards of the Game 7
Dick Button: Olympic Skating Championship 8
Inspiration 9
Paul Wylie, "JFK" 10
Trying to Escape 11
The Blaze 12
Rosalynn Competes on a Las Vegas Night 13
Roses in the Night 14
Cirque de Soleil 15
Schindler's List 16
The Cat 17
Yagudin Struggles 18
Blood Chilled as Borscht 19
Avec du Song 20
Gift of Ice 21
No Lesser Metals 22
Color of Roses 23
Fierceness under Control 24
You Skate: for Tanith Belbin 25
I'm Too Sexy 26
Night Skate 27
Sugarplum Fairy 28
And the Moon Spilled Down 29

Minutes of Pearl

Moon sifts down,
cool breath of a goddess.

In silks we whirl with snowflakes—
dissolving jewels—
as a piano somewhere
creates a dancing tempo.

Together we drift through a hundred
years of stars
before flying across frozen tears.

Minutes of gold, ivory, steel

We twirl, ecstatic, savoring each moment
to make it last
aware of the flaxen-haired child of our love,
aware of each other's faces.

Minutes of diamond, silver, vermillion

We exchange smiles.
He holds me on his powerful shoulders.
Once hard as icicles
our rhythms have long since
melted into one.

*For Katya and Sergei Grinkov, Olympics pairs skaters,
many gold medals; husband and wife (husband died at age 29)

Boccelli Sings; Boitano Skates

And his voice was wings, white fire,
foaming wine
while the skater leaped
with its rising.
He sang like fire
as the skater flew down ice
colored like cool orchids
and the moon whispered in Italian:
Bella…amore.
His voice held bells, incandescence,
holy flame
and the skater whirled, vaulted,
slid on one knee on silk ice.
The piano chanted and charmed the moonlight
flowing like champagne
or death or birth;
Andrea Boccelli watched
golden angel
while Boitano spun himself
into heaven
and back to earth.

(Brian Boitano: an American figure skater,
 Olympic gold medalist)

First Grand Prix Victory: Sasha Cohen
(Rachmaninoff, Piano Concerto #2)

Violins' long wings escort her
onto the floor. Piano keys blur
into white moons like the spotlights.

Ballet habits lift the skater's legs
into fouettes, her arms into rosettes.
Fear falls from her like an old shawl
and she dances in chiffon dress.
Arpeggio: she kicks to fast beats
then in a waterfall of strong notes
she creates curlicues of footwork
like ornate gold earrings of a countess.

Piano thunders from deep in the Russian soul
of Rachmaninoff. After a running butterfly
Sasha slips into a spin, vanishing yet never
vanishing like the composers of past ages.
Violins cry, fly like fierce glittering birds,
sing in unknown lyrical languages.

In a spiral, the skater's legs extend further,
further, higher,
back to her ancestors from the Ukraine—
she extends them to victory.

Lady of the Ice
> *for Michelle Kwan*

Mist castled in shadows,
as the skater dreamed herself into life,
holding the world at far distance
with a wave of silver-tipped fingers.

She spins closing her eyes
while a white bird melts into her breast.

Violins gallop, flying with her down frost,
held back by silk reins. Her dress grows
long and silken as her body changes
to that of a woman.

A leap!
Light as a magic wand,
she whirls through cool air,
then lands without a sound on ice—
an ermine robe, spread huge and long.

Follow me, she says, *follow my trail,*
until moonlight fades in the arms of dawn.
Dance in my footsteps
as clocks click like glass slippers,
and I fall into the music: my prince, my own.

Flying over Paris
for Sonja Henie

On an airplane she lay in the arms of her husband
and reminisced about the facets of her life:
enormous Papa who doted on her, bought her skates,
guided her to the first Olympic gold.
Fearlessly she scampered over scintillating ice,
flung herself into an axle, whirled in white skirts.
With poise she faced the glare of cameras
knowing Papa was at her side. She smiled
as she leaped over precarious silver frost,
ignoring wicked green grins of little rival girls.
Her body—young and strong—did not let her down.

On an airplane, dozing on her way to Oslo
from Paris, she dreamed of past days:
a third Olympic gold, a dress tailored just for her:
white silk, ermine. Pushing Daryl Zanuck
into a corner…dancing in the dazzle of Hollywood
on the hunt for a million diamonds—that special
sparkle unique in gems.

Brilliant cut to: a spiral on one foot, pas de deux
in an ice show ("Pavlova on Ice"). A funeral (Papa),
big bouquet of lilies, still face, stiff upper lip.
Glittering with Tyrone Power, herself in diaphanous gown.
Emerging from a Rolls-Royce with two elkhounds,
before darting into an arena in gold tights, sun-lit scarf,
yellow flash of a canary diamond.

So many smiles, glittering and apparently
indestructible as a diadem.
Marriage to a third husband, childhood sweetheart.

He did not tell her the last diagnosis.
On an airplane from Paris to Norway
she did not know she would die in his arms.

Dangerous Skate
for Kurt Browning

Ice—I cannot stop
her tricks and teasing.
She whirls up toward me
a dark face
veiled in ghostly white.
I waltz yet her slick
hands make me tango
while she glitters at me
in a mysterious smile.
Dance! Dance!
her cold tongue demands
and I whirl and twirl,
run and leap as the music
commands us to go on.
Spin! I swirl in wild
fire of the rhythms, as frost
burns my feet
and I nearly fall
into the arms of the black-eyed girl.

(Kurt Browning: world-class skater;
could never win Olympics medal for Canada)

Hazards of the Game
Oksana Baiul, Orphan Skater

Shadowed by dark knights of rivals,
she advances over ice.
Lynx-trimmed memories swirling around her,
she dances alone with darkness, Tchaikovsky,
and beloved old tales edged in gilt.
Pressures pant
at her heels, wolf-tongued, glowing red.
She leaps,
held up by one spark of faith
and the sudden arm of her ghostly mother.
In a square of safety
Oksana lands,
as her mother kneels in a corner and prays.

Fears quelled,
the skater turns from pawn to queen
spiraling in satin, to a burst of applause.
Spotlights wander in purple plumes
that waver and roll away, blurring her focus.
Other slim figures
watch trembling from the side.
Her skates castling
the precarious floor,
she skips past a jagged edge.

Dick Button
    Olympic Skating Championship

He charges down the ivory ice
blood swirling through bright cheeks

The wings of youthful will lift high
and beat along his back

Skilled feet move fast
to make all rivals look like doves

Panting whirling gliding
without a single pause

Skates steel themselves to ride
and blaze like diamonds over glass

Fine fire in every bone, the fire cries
for power to breathe eternally

Unyielding will beats strong
he plunges into perfect spins

merging with the blaze of music
and hope of breathless crowds

then flies above the coffin of ice
gravity left below him as a corpse

Inspiration
> *for Dorothy Hamill*

Silver roses of the ice, petals cool and still
provide the bed from which she springs
delicate and fragrant

Ghosts with slender limbs—Sonya, Peggy—
breathe life into her silent, trembling soul
as she flies down dreaming frost

Each arm a perfect world
she spins in whispers of mysterious grace
blossoming pure white

Her spiral blends with wind and fantasy
to waken buds of other girls
for other flights

Toward royal red of sun she leaps and whirls
then is blown down to the ice
a bouquet thrown

Violins call; she stands up with a dewy smile
unfurls again her perfect pose
floats lightly as a miracle

So that hopes rise wherever petals fall

Paul Wylie, "JFK"

Every move sculpted
Every turn planned

A small figure in solemn black
cuts the cold air like a knife

each spin perfect
each kick high

running across ice he grows larger
as he slides into the grand music

Powerful arms pull us into the scene
Legs muscular, unyielding, hunt for truth

With gusto he feels each beat
Bends to each mood of the brass
   Tragic, victorious

Fights against odds
In shadows   turns and turns

He carves the story in the frost and wind
Carves another life across ice

Carves his greatness into memory
Carves himself into history

Trying to Escape

Spotlights claw down
from the ceiling. Ice
soft as scent. She
must have a win.

In shadows gray as guns,
as uniforms, she hits
the ground running.
Behind her stands a rival,
dress shining dangerously
as three-leafed ivy.
Katerina shoots
across the floor, dead set
on a jump. She flies,
nearly falls, grits her teeth
and lands on her feet.

Each moment a challenge,
each musical bar a trap,
she whirls, spreading long
arms, aiming with each inch
of femininity.

Out of the blackness of the past,
out of the cage of conformity,
out of the unmoving steel
of communism, she blasts
in silk, in lipstick and powder
smiling to cover desperation
on ice rough and
dangerous as barbed wire.

(Katerina Witt had to win Olympic gold
in order to be granted freedom
by communist East Germany.)

The Blaze
Yuka Sato and Jason Dongeon

They skate together,
each flame liquid enough
to blend with another flame.
Flaring, dancing, flowing,
flinging, mingling
they slide so close
on ice of rose and ruby glaze.

Two flames cannot destroy each other;
one makes the other bigger.
Burning away distances between them
burning away logs of discord or doubt,
they fly;
golden, yielding to bliss,
rising to the urge to trust,
they curl together
more fragile than satin or a violin
as fragile as magic.

Rosalynn Competes on a Las Vegas Night
for Rosalynn Sumners, Olympic Silver Medalist

Muscled, blonde, she carves her name on ice
taking control of the crowd.
Beneath her the frost lies in a blur
like scattered playing cards.

Dark the shadows and black her gown
as precisely she covers slick ice.
She leaps in a toss of sensuous limbs
while drum-beats rattle like dice.

A perfume of nocturnes, a dance on sharp knives,
a whirling—no moments to spare—
the moonlight dizzied by a fizz of fast moves
in white and blinding air.

She flies through the wildly expanding rink
cold as the steel of a gun.
Stars cartwheel toward her chardonnay smile
as she closes the night with a win.

Roses in the Night
    for Tanith Belbin

Roses in the night and raspberries
    shining on the beautiful river,
the skater dances over a dream of water;
secrets wait hidden inside slide trombones
and the piccolo prances only to be forgotten.

Distant lights glide softly as a whisper
    in an ear,
stars wheel on an invisible axel,
piano notes fly up and glisten on the moon,
the skater floats held up only by love.

Cirque de Soleil
for Nicole Bobek

She skates in a mask to music blended with cries
of birds. She slides over a tightrope on which
loss is on the left side. Her body is lithe
and lovely as a magician's wife.

She skates to pull herself back out of a runaway
season of loss. High above us, she teeters,
tries a tour de force. Success!
Her rope is a melting icicle.

One leg extends as she shows acrobatic flexibility.
Her ballet movements continue in a
smooth line yet she fights against a
fall. Defeat waits below, cold as ice.

Night-rope that can break like a dream of riding
a horse on a swinging bridge over a surging
black river. Nicole whirls and nearly sinks.
Saves herself, an inch from the dark.

Nicole skates in a silk mask to bare white fingers
of a piano. She hops over a knot of fear
and bypasses loss on the abyss. She spins
hugging one leg stretched way above her head.

In the end, she's on the ice, doing splits,
her body charmed and musical, white as fantasy
or milky stars in a tent of mist, and vanishing…
like a magician's wife.

"Schindler's List"
Skated by Paul Wylie

Ash-mauve slacks dark shirt
   in a dim cold room

Strong arm sweeps away doubts
   Loss is not an option

Determination pulls him
Music drags him into its train

High kicks express a strong longing
   to become part of an old story

Hiding inside the fast blur of spins
Blue spotlights try to pin him down

Dashes, whirls beat of perilous music
In its clutches he becomes for now a victim

Down on one knee
No runner could turn turn turn so fast

A brilliant shadow
   he flees through the night

Outlasting others pushing to the limit
   in a black breathless barb-wired flight

He is more than a skater
He is history

Cannot escape greatness
Cannot escape victory

The Cat

Cat eyes in the dark
filled with night's strangeness.
She runs away
wearing her freedom
without apology. Far off
she pounces on some animal
slinking toward her
from the shadowed alley.

Cat eyes flicker in nearby bushes
reflecting the distant moon.
Alone in a world
menaced by strangeness
she devours her own fears.
She wants to be fed and stroked
yet lurks under dark trees. Slowly she
approaches on fancy feet.

Cat eyes
filled with fire and loneliness
of long purple hours.
Lover of the half-lit evening,
cheek frosted
by the moon's cool breath.
She whirls
hoping for admiration
lifting an elegant neck
in a regal pose.

(Katerina Witt escaped from East Germany
to become a famous Olympics figure skater.)

Yagudin Struggles
Olympics Epic

Rink whirls like the spin
of a fortuneteller's globe.
He wheels trying to stand on skates
in spite of flu. Pushing, fighting
he races past the bleachers
faces blurring like tarot cards.

Maybe these scissor kicks will knock out
feelings of weakness. The smiling memory
of his mother holds him together
like the yeast and eggs in her fragrant
black bread. Alexei circles,
the reds and blues of fans' jackets
melting and blending like a gypsy's
flaring skirt.

He leaps and hopes the hand of Fate
is courteous enough to help
him down. Yes—
yet on the next jump
she deserts him.

Fallen on the ice
he stares at a crack
like his life line:
huge and strong
and headed toward victory
sometime in the clouded future.

Blood Chilled as Borscht
for Evgeny Pleshenko

Ice like peeled onions
I dance to folk tunes
distinctively Russian

Whirling in flared sleeves
and embroidered vest
I leap to show them
my country is best

I skate with bravado
with blue and red flair
My great land has given me
gusto to spare

If I leave for a few days
my heart remembers
those far snowy steppes
of a deep long December

My soul has become shaped
like a bright golden dome
of the fairytale churches
of my beautiful home

« Avec Du Song »
Skated by Josee Chouinard

Her feet sigh over aquamarine ice.
She immerses herself in music
that caresses her face for this
one night. Josee wears a light blush
named peche charme. In an arabesque
she pursues her affaire d'amour
with an evasive Muse.

Everything is precarious:
the glowing beryl below her feet,
hands that gentle on a violin,
apricot glow of spotlights.
Slick slender wand of the glassy clock
stills time for a moment,
and allows Josee to skate
through an arch, passing beyond shyness.

Gliding overture into a leap—
a ballet flight in air. She lands on one
ivory foot; dances to piano keys
made of white rose petals. Her skates
tell us an ancient tale
as she turns and revolves, reverently
following each pattern of classical flirtation.

She spins, whirls faster, faster,
turning into a blurred silk cape,
or a vision of snowy gloves,
or a feathery ballroom fan…

Gift of the Ice

I am music
I am a diamond over diamonds
I am fire

Like shadows on snow
I glide   I spiral
while violins dance with me
Flying, quicksilver as in my dreams
then the slide into a death-drop spin
Ice glitters, giving me power
if it does not destroy me
does not break me
Ice lends me elegant fire
Quickly in blue mirrors
ice carries me
toward my desire

No Lesser Metals
> *for Evan Lysacek*

The light lands bright
on fragile ice

The fear is real
So is the power

No suggestion of bronze
A streak—white teeth, fiery satin
A roar across the frost

Pressure descends
So do the drums

No suggestion of silver
Heart pounds as fists clench for first
High and higher refuse to lose
Doubt flees from leaps
Holding back no more, to whirl and twist

Only gold must flash
Only the fire, the lion, and the lasting flame

"The Color of Roses"
—*Skated by Yuka Sato*

Small and oriental
bending like a flower

She floats in air
granted wings by a fairy godmother

When she turns
white petals whisper of symmetry
of play and reverie

She spins
her dress the color of things
weightless and vanishing

Only the 5-petaled fragrance of love
on ice holding peace like a wild rose

Music the hue of a prism
drifting in mist

Only the body keeps time

Soul flies
in a piano-splash of leaps
and gleams

Only the ones who believe
ever see what they dream

Fierceness under Control
Elvis Stojko

The snake of lightning, tamed,
curls up inside the moon.

Spurs of the stars
fall down and spark the skater
to jump high.

Anger and frustration
harnessed and trained
give Elvis momentum.
Why must Canada always
come in second?
He skates in pain.

Night winds join with the music,
turn the evening into a dream.
Obediently each player
keeps perfect time. Calmness
and concentration live in large
silent, electric-lighted houses
called muscles, through habits
of karate and tai chi.

Night animals stop killing
each other. A jaguar
disciplined and black
rises in Elvis's soul,
drives him to attack
the triple combinations
that allow him to survive.

(Elvis Stojko: award-winning Canadian skater)

You Skate
> *for Tanith Belbin*

Red lights turn the shining floor
to maraschino cherries.

Life bursts free to glide
and masquerade as immortal.

Quick dancing to a maraca beat—
Ice gleams beneath like marquetry.

You spin into a firefly…
wings growing large and gold.

Leaping, you let go fears, reach through clouds,
hair flying like an angel.

Oh soar, fast rhythms, never drop
while stars give birth to other stars,

The only gravity still to defeat
lies far away beyond the Moon.

"I'm Too Sexy"
Victor Petrenko Skates

I'm too sexy for my skin,
        Too sexy with my grin,
        As sexy as Americans—
            Just sexy!

Hey—I desire to clown & dance,
      Giggle
      Wiggle
      Prance

I'm fired up, I'll be a star
longer than I can drive a car
Watch me watch me
        Not from afar

Hey! I love you, love each fan
All my life I want to be young
        want to be a danger

Feel my sex appeal,
I could kiss all of you,
I'm in love with these lights
        like a bed full of tangerines

I'm the sexiest man alive,
I'm the one who savors life,
The more you clap the more I know
        this vodka's gone to my brain

I'm too sexy
      Watch me spin
      Watch my grin
      Watch me double & triple my fun

Night Skate
for Nicole Bobek

I remember the chiffon in the shadows,
and the blue roses that fell from it.
Thunder of the blue dimness,
waking the dangerous ice—a
great shark. The skater, slender as a
shiver, falls, her dress billowing around her
like a chill pool. She survives by the
teeth of her skates, digging in,
every muscle willing to fight. Birds
fly overhead, shadowing her face.
Midnight and the skates like twinned
mirrors of moonlight, violins sleek as seals,
the pounding of drums.

Deeper in the memory, the pale white
rocks, faint lightning trying to warn,
while ice rises up to feed on
four young men.

But this night the moon washes
all tragedy into the sea, and the skater
now glides through air that is cool and
boneless, incapable of injury.

Sugarplum Fairy
for Peggy Fleming

She blends with the white ice, gleaming
in a million crystals; her silver dress
floats in snowflakes to the slightest
breath of woodwinds. Her soul melts,
spills out to the audience,
freezes into a diamond.

Overhead, the moon has been crushed
and re-sculpted into our deepest dreams
of a prince on a milky trail.
Frost gleams, misting from rose to green.
And she turns, turns, in the hands
of Tchaikovsky, who gave us the delirium
of heaven-sent beauty. Blending with his violins
she grants us the life of a princess,
that leads everyone
into a land airy and timeless.

And the Moon Spilled Down
  for Katya Gordeeva

some of its memories
and fed us moonfires
with a silver spoon.

In black, the skater spiraled
lost in a labyrinth
of the past.

Ivory joys she gave us,
as she danced and flew,
telling us of darkness and light,
of dreams trapped in ice,
desires throbbing deep
inside a piano, the new
unstained silk of violins, the white
around each eye no matter
what age or color,
the miracle of first flight.

Mardelle Fortier has over 100 poems in print, in journals such as *Rhino* and *Chicago Literary Review* (University of Chicago). In 2013, Finishing Line Press published her first poetry chapbook, *WHITE FIRE*. *MOON FIRE* continues with more poems from the author's lifelong love of skating. An award-winning poet, she has won many prizes, especially from Poets and Patrons of Chicago, which finally awarded her the top prize (Best of the Best). She has held various offices in Illinois State Poetry Society, including president. Fortier also participated in Poets Club of Chicago and other literary organizations. For about seven years, she has worked as poetry and fiction editor for *DuPage Valley Review*, a magazine dedicated to promoting the arts in DuPage County and sponsored by Benedictine University. Sharing her enjoyment of writing with students, and helping them to find a wider audience, she has taught at various Chicagoland colleges (Loyola, North Central, Benedictine, for example). Currently she teaches creative writing (including novels, stories, memoirs as well as poetry) at College of DuPage.